She
Becomes
Time

She
Becomes
Time

.

Margaret Randall

WingsPress

San Antonio, Texas
2016

First Edition

ISBN: 978-1-60940-509-0 (paperback original)

E-books:

epub: 978-1-60940-510-6
Mobipocket/Kindle: 978-1-60940-511-3
Library PDF: 978-1-60940-512-0

Wings Press
627 E. Guenther
San Antonio, Texas 78210
Phone/fax: (210) 271-7805
On-line catalogue and ordering:
www.wingspress.com

Wings Press books are distributed to the trade by
Independent Publishers Group
www.ipgbook.com

Library of Congress Cataloging-in-Publication Data:

Randall, Margaret, 1936- author.
  She becomes time / Margaret Randall.
First Edition. | San Antonio, Texas : Wings Press, 2016.
ISBN 9781609405090 (paperback) | ISBN 9781609405113 (kindle/
mobipocket ebook) | ISBN 9781609405120 (library pdf)
Subjects: | BISAC: POETRY / American / General.

LCC PS3535.A56277 A6 2016
811/.54--dc23
LC record available at http://lccn.loc.gov/2016004854

As Always, for Barbara

"Who we are when we are not love has always caused us shame."

"When I say now that I'm done being dead I have declared an alternative self."

"When is the tipping point?"

—Akilah Oliver[1]

Contents

Mexico

Cuba

She
Becomes
Time

All Destination

I resign myself without Everest,
without wandering Kathmandu
or sipping tea at a Bali cafe.

Never learned Mandarin,
read Rilke in German
or wrote a successful novel.

Never hiked the Inca Trail
to the Gate of the Sun,
a dream nurtured into my 75th year.

Four children, ten grandchildren
and one great grandchild
leave me struggling to keep up.

And the loss I share with so many
who couldn't make a world
worthy of our progeny.

The greater dream waves
its ledger, two columns
of checkmarks noting

journeys taken, places I stood
and those I will not
touch or change.

More adventurous than some
or more determined,
I climbed into Rapa Nui's crater

to caress immense stone figures
undone for centuries.
I slipped through Petra's siq.

Language holds me
on its powerful wings,
offers to take me in any direction.

I reach for your hand, love,
curl my fingers in yours.
All destination breathes in their heat.

First Family

One Memory Less Among the Weeds

If older sister had lived more than hours,
a lifetime or other circumstance,
I wouldn't have a second-hand name
I cherish as my own.

If Grandpa hadn't taken what wasn't his
with Grandma looking on,
if salty and sweet hadn't come
to the party with intent to confuse.

If the young Italian lover had closed
the bathroom door, an image
more relevant than Ivory soap,
one memory less among the weeds.

What if blue and green had always
danced with one another,
red and orange burst into flame
on the walls of a child's room.

I cannot say if reading that passage at eight
about the concentration camp, then slamming
shut the book and furtively opening it again
was childhood curiosity or awe.

War was always huge, unknown and battering,
Bundles for Britain followed by marching
endlessly from there to here.
I carried placards, then thirty extra pounds.

If I hauled words in my firstborn's diaper bag
or reinvented them
everywhere I stayed
more than a few exploratory months,

it was a complication born of poetry and war,
following a broken arrow
to weather, language,
and humor disguised as rice and beans.

In Vietnam I found broken clamshells
on a pontoon moving across a river
where bridges and bombs took turns
and I wore USA: trembling question mark.

I kept on moving, collecting teachers
and battlegrounds,
more children with open eyes,
their fathers hovering.

And then I stopped, embraced by the one
I was meant to find who was meant
to find me. I tell her these stories
night by night in a single breath.

Being their Daughter

It was the question without an answer.
Sometimes her silence
was gunmetal gray,
sometimes rimmed in orchid pink.

He didn't know and didn't want to know.
Like most couples, they had their problems.
Being their daughter
didn't provide a clue.

DNA isn't part of this story.
Each year I ask
in the voice of a younger me
and reap an answer of rainbows.

People always told me I had big bones
like him. My resemblance to her
stared back in every mirror.
They're both gone now,

leaving me a story winding down,
repeating echoes
and resignation
transparent as morning sky.

Where I Live and Die

I am in the picture frame but look
as if I want out.
The relative behind the shutter
must have urged
come on now smile,
may have displayed impatience
at my lack of interest, refusal
to take my place in his tableaux.

Almost eight decades have passed.
The image is faded, edges frayed
beyond their pinked irregularity
defining that home album era.
I cannot remember what lay beyond
the picture plane,
what truth or action
social formality stole.

What I do know is what I longed for then
without knowing its name
I have grabbed with both hands
and pulled onto this map
where I live and die
along with all those
who invited me
inside looking in.

Like a Bull in a China Shop

I rise, astonished by air beneath my floating limbs,
buoyant dance of a body my father once said
was like a bull in a china shop: grade school
ballet recital yearning for grace.

Grace would never be my strong suite but
here I am skimming the top bookshelf
where poetry flashes before my eyes, pulling
my feet way up and in to avoid stubbed toes.

The platform chair rocks back and forth,
no one settled on its curved seat,
not even a ghost hiding its presence
to watch this carefree dance.

Faster and faster I race beneath a ceiling
threatening sudden stop, untouched,
propelled by some magical force:
three parts helium, one part abhorrence of war.

Pied Piper of love and logic, I sound the first
totally on-key melody of my life
and beckon the world to follow,
peace so much easier than this sad default.

Mother and the Mac Truck

Mother sat erect, her hands firmly
grasping ten and two
and always drove
a good twenty miles slower
than the speed limit,

which is why in my dream
I was surprised
she was speeding
and swerving all over the road,
even onto its broken shoulder.

I tried to grab the wheel but she was
determined to make it
to the yellow stucco hospital—
a building like the old French ones
I saw in Hanoi, 1974.

She needed medication. I held
a lab envelope that may have
contained her shit
in the hand not concerned
with steadying the wheel.

She really confused me, though,
when she briefly became
a teenage delinquent male

I was trying to hide
from the police.

I smoothed his hair, tucked him
into bed and promised
I wouldn't let them get him.
He smiled gratefully, begging
over and over *please keep me safe*.

All I knew about the boy was
he'd stolen a Mac truck.
Then it was Mother
who'd stolen the truck
and the kid had a plan

to give it back. I woke thinking
my mother's shit shouldn't
have been too heavy for me to carry,
and Law and Order wreaks terror
everywhere in this New World Order.

Broken Cities

and

Perfect Cubes

A Day Like This

On a night like this my nine-year-old son
discovered the stars through the telescope
at Cuba's tiny observatory
where a young Russian astronomer
put her eye to the instrument
and heart to the universe
every sultry Caribbean night.
His first apprenticeship.

Forty years ago on a day like this
my ten year old daughter
stood on a chair,
a wooden pointer in her hand, authority in her voice.
Her classmates listened
as she explained New Math,
traveled a path that wouldn't split
for decades, questioning
her destination on the run.

On a day like this we gathered peacefully
at Mexico City's Plaza of Three Cultures,
circle of concrete apartment blocks
and righteous colonial church
built over ruins of Aztec glory.
Loudspeakers carried the rousing static
of speeches until gunfire tossed bodies
in piles of before and after,

turned history on itself.
On a day like this but not at all like this
we began to understand
the shameful color of betrayal,
where kindness hides itself
and for how long,
why a Vietnamese monk lit himself on fire
and died without a twitch of muscle,
no sound but the hiss of flame.

On a day like and unlike today
we remember the child who speaks
surrounded by silence,
farmers coaxing potatoes from vertical plots
on Andean mountainsides,
a girlchild leaning into her loom
in the dim light of an Egyptian factory,
and the tiny desert flower that blooms
from its bed of rock-hard earth.

A day like this has nowhere to go
but home.
Uneasy, it inhabits its calendar
—Long Count, Hebrew, Anno Domini,
Consular or Gregorian—
tries to hide in a robust month,
escape tumultuous weather,
cherish younger siblings
and avoid the rage of those who

do no honor to a day like this.

Their Braided Fingers

—for Mary Oishi

I didn't get to be a scientist, not this time around.
My creative impulse never would have borne
the slow angst of double-blind studies
or impartial observation.
Still, my poet's intuition
brings me to the same place.

Your grandma's terror during the firebombing of Tokyo
adheres to my DNA,
the epigenetic change it hosts
reflects a grandfather kidnapped from his African village
while I no longer remember
an uncle I should have been able to trust
fingering my childhood.

The point is, none of these genetic memories
nor childhoods are lost.
They reside in our cellular memory,
the genetic material of which we're made.
Their braided fingers will not let our double helix go.

Time's Language

*Light does not get old: a photon that emerged from
the Big Bang is the same age today as it was then.
There is no passage of time at light speed.*

—Brian Greene[4]

Time appears in its loose-fitting shift,
knocks on the child's windowpane,
hopscotches gleefully
then drags itself across the floor
for the unbearable wait.

Midlife it sizzles, careens against walls,
stumbles over roadblocks
trying out new dance steps
but catching its voluminous cloak
on all that excess furniture.

In age I hardly notice its devious passage,
steady breath lifting me through night.
Caressing my shoulders it launches
the occasional taunt
or hides in a double take of mirrors.

Sometimes it catches me off guard, sometimes
I want to tell it: *slow down, dammit!*
Sometimes I nestle in its arms
and understand its tempo
perfectly.

Bead of an Elephant's Eye

The silences are heaviest
when great events
like the birth of a child
or stubborn resistance
against whatever torture
turn weightless along the way.

My children broke loose where
the road split
and I stopped for a moment
uncertain which fork
pronounced my name.
The next generation always cheers us on.

We share that single destination
and I can offer you a ride
but will not carry your baggage.
Inheritance locked in secrets
always weighs too much.
Shoulder yours and travel with me.

I've learned what I cannot do
weighs more than all I did.
What slips through my fingers
leaves imprints of desert dust.
Peeling the secrets as we go
will laugh us safely home.

This found life—our great love—
rides effortlessly
between breastbone and diaphragm.
Details make the journey:
an almost forgotten conversation
or bead of an elephant's eye.

Joining of No Return

Where rock meets rock along the jagged cleft
above Pueblo Bonito's back wall,
where brick floats upon mythic emptiness
in Hagia Sofia's great dome,
where calligraphy is coaxed to art
when image is forbidden above the entranceway
to an abandoned way station—*caravansarai*—
and the Silk Road sorts its memories,
there is a joining of no return.

There is nothing messy about these seams,
nothing left over.
A waning sun turns the Nile's expanding ripples
to brief ridges of copper light
as the same sun turns wave fields on the Mekong,
Irrawaddy, or Colorado an equivalent hue.
Yet all waves belong only to themselves
and along the lines where each river laps its shore
a thin line separates seeing from unknowing.

Such borders drip salt on slightly parted lips,
images embed themselves
in soft age-mottled flesh.
Great stones placed by the Inca
in perfect harmony
issue words I feared I might forget.

Each migration held by invisible mortar
imprints itself on this landscape
unfolding upon my tongue.

Where your skin and mine knit tight
between your right breast
and my left,
our bodies fit together perfectly,
and despite our sudden hot-flash blooms
touch speaks its language of years.
Here every cell brings memory home,
every nerve ending rests:
the boundary along which we grow.

Not Your Neighborhood

For Anne Waldman on her 70th birthday. Poet of poets.

It's not your neighborhood at first but a street
across town where balconies of flowers
become grotesque fragments
trampled in choking dust. Another family's children
maimed or dead. Another searching
for shelter. Where are they? Right there, and then
everywhere as the last slivers of silence disappear.

Your side of the city falls, landscape of rubble, work
and school are lost, then water and food.
And now you are walking, walking
with what you can carry
and every day you carry less.
Direction your only friend, its destination
enveloped in something you once called hope.

The rest of the world—those families who still have
clean rooms with televisions parsing
the nightly news—sees the face of a small girl
with large eyes, her curls reach mid-thigh
of the adult beside her, who is beyond the frame.
They are moving north and west. You are
moving but not as fast

and the small girl with large eyes is not enough
to wake a complacent world. So another
picture tries: a man gently lifting

the body of a dead child from the sea.
In minutes the image gets a million *likes*,
instagram attention from those
who watch in warmth from rainproof homes.

Tens of thousands crowd rubber dinghies or creaking
boats, follow rail tracks, storm borders,
escaping countries dissolving in blood and dust,
carrying those who cannot walk, pushing
wheelchairs, pulling carts. Few are photogenic
or speak sufficient English
to muster sympathy on the six o'clock news.

As all sides fight on, countries lose the definition
of country and the thugs remain convinced
they must fight harder, kill more,
destroy memory along with those who live
in its fragile wake. *Fight to the finish* is a dictate
designed to make sure
everything dies, even the beloved stories.

Twenty-first century paints itself in colors
rent by razor wire, money demanded
by those always ready to profit from misery,
obscure words to be learned,
new tastes to swallow as arms reach out
with woolen gloves and teddy bears.
Exhaustion devours what used to fit perfectly.

Most of the faces aren't engaging enough,
most of the eyes not large and round.

Most of the bodies are bent, never the best
camera angle, most cannot speak English.
The small girl who is still alive
and the dead child's body washed ashore
share a heavy load. They labor beyond their years.

In Broken Cities

In ancient Syria, Arzu and Azizos
the gods of evening
and morning stars,
cast equal light upon a land
headed for death.

Quetzalcoatl and Tezcalipoca
cannot question
their gender roles
when conquest leaves them
battering want.

Apollo and Artemis still stumble
through time.
Castor is mortal
to the divinity of Pollux.
Egypt tells us Geb is of earth
while Nut surveys unruly heavens.

Data's positronic brain
makes computational magic
while his malignant twin Lore,
possessing the emotion chip,
fatally wounds his maker.
The Star Trek character teaches us
reality and humanity are not the same.

Identical twins of war and gluttony
stretch love to the breaking point,
rip hope to insignificant particles:
breadcrumbs looking for a path.

A word flies in like the dove of peace,
settles briefly in my hair
relieves its nervous bowel
then disappears
in a temper of wings.

Those few who remain
after terror wipes the map
of all but a landscape of rebar,
are lost supplicants
in broken cities.

They try to decipher the word,
to bring it home,
but cannot decide
if it is syllable or logogram,
noun or verb.

Still they hoist it
on reverent shoulders
eager to begin again,
to rise from the ashes of shame
as civilization's grandly decorated bullies.

Gleaming and Dark

Long lines of captives climbed those pyramid steps,
some drugged, honored, others resigned,
unable to accept the brutal rite.
Up above, priests fixed their bodies to an altar
while others used sharp flint knives,
opened them gut to breastbone
and lifted their still beating hearts to the gods:
a sacrificial offering, plea for renewal
regeneration of a culture
whose pageantry and art excite us still.

Patriotic fervor convinces today's more willing captives
their job is to keep us free, protect our security
while earning a paycheck in hard times.
Those they are sent to kill, after all, are not like us,
mock our exceptionalism,
flew stolen planes into our mightiest buildings.
A child who confuses that scrap of metal with a toy
and the wedding party making its way
across a desert where love goes up in smoke:
collateral damage all, war's painful cost.

Ritual death was the fate of those enslaved by Aztec lords,
food for gods who renewed each morning's sun.
For our Empire's soldiers
body armor may save torsos
while legs explode and heads close over eternal hell.

Thousands come home in flag-wrapped coffins,
others finish themselves with alcohol, drugs,
or the peace a self-inflicted bullet brings.
They've earned a country's gratitude
but vulnerability is risky for the fighting man.

Flags fill airport terminals, handmade signs and
pale children welcome the warriors home.
In city streets and shopping malls
the rest of us thank them for their service,
remember an earlier war
when we confused those boys with policy,
rank and file with criminal masterminds.
Memory lives in a broad black granite V:
gleaming and dark
as the obsidian of those ancient knives.

Someone We Do Not Recognize Stares Back

Damp haze presses down on ordinary moments,
how your extended palm feels against mine
as we meet and greet,
where the mudslide erases a village,
bigotry in the news anchor's voice
when he calls one opponent State
and the other "a militant group"
although both are democratically elected
and equally concerned
with fending off the shelling of babies.
Too much salt in your potato salad,
too much benzene in our water.

We construct a scale of values,
carefully order our lives
to reflect concentric circles: war
several rings within gardens,
profit sustaining a center point
and art hanging on for dear life at edges
rising in waves crashing almost beyond our reach.
What she made. What he made.
What we make
of what all of us have made
as we gaze in the mirror and someone
we do not recognize stares back.

Now We See Them, Now We Don't

A family walks down a canyon wash
bordered by paintbrush and sage.
They carry children and grinding stones,
one water jug, one corrugated dish
fashioned last year by grandmother's hands.

Grandmother because she remembers
the last great flood: water
swelling the creek just below First Balcony,
knows the way because she holds
the stories, follows the rains.

Family because lineage, community
woven into days and then nights,
alignment of landscape,
people carrying their lives
like seed banks of future.

Travel because a road, a time, a pulse
of tidal migration, their route
in meridian memory,
their lungs expand and contract
through geologic time.

Return etched into pathways
of sand and wind,
images pecked into rock,
land that rises and falls
beneath their hungers.

Twelve sixty-two by our poor reckoning.
Now we see them,
now we don't:
human figures moving along roads
we can only follow from the sky

and only then in those fragments
of vision we still possess
when able to put aside the fear
our arrogance requires
in order to keep us from knowing

where ancestors traveled, where
their children will go
after they come back,
tethered to canyons
and stars.

Look Up

Somersaulting across canyon slots
flying wall to wall
carrying sheets of desert varnish
to drape from narrow ledges
where ancestors stored corn
for winter's uncertainty.

Against those silent walls
you still see bodies
within bodies,
snake or lightning bolt,
mountain sheep in profile,
proud horns aligned for the fight.

Perhaps this is where you
are meant to look up,
turn left,
wedge your own body
from toe and finger hold
into a single perfect maneuver,

the one that will take you back 1300 years
to where they breathed,
worked, laughed
inside a circle of world
where the stitches sewing sky to earth
fail us now.

What misstep ripped time's seam,
tearing solution
from cause and effect,
placed multiple choices
in our hands
when two were more than enough?

When did time begin to move
faster than cosmic cycles,
a new story beginning
before its predecessor
had a chance to stop, rest,
remember its name?

Between Here and Then

—for Pam Nomura

When they traveled they brought their center
with them, anchored a world
oblivious to Greece or Rome, couldn't know
camels lumbered beyond an unimagined ocean
and other humans also walked this earth.

Jaguar's eye still stares from the mountaintop,
steps still climb the wall of rock
losing themselves in sky.
We cannot decipher the etched spiral
or know who carved its message.

It wasn't vacation (such a modern concept)
but need: rain and more generous soil,
winds cooling rather than scorching,
weather that could be a friend
or places dreamt by the gentlest spirit.

Play surely existed, a quiver of joy
or joke shared with family
reaching to fill the empty spaces,
cradling silence
on its creased face.

When your center slips between here and then
or hides in the folds
of dreams others dreamt for you,
dare dream your own.
Memory will reward you with yourself.

The Memories of Others

She couldn't climb aboard
the memories of others
and travel as we do.

No museums, no books
to nurture dreams,
need her tradition.

Nearby stories crouched
in the space of her only life
until figures pecked in stone

whispered dance and hunt
before the sun came up
or starlight pooled her eyes.

She knew nothing of counting days
from the maybe birth
of a man who never walked

in her small dreams,
didn't know her year
would be called CE 800.

Ice cracked to softer air
warming her bones,
then delicate green tendrils

offered squash and beans
to be eaten fresh
or dried for the next freeze

that would come as surely
as her skin's loosening
and the slowing of her step.

Seasons inspired blood,
their comings and goings
spread across her horizon:

gifts of worry and life
required every instinct
of experience.

Today we rely on different gifts:
the memories of others,
invent infallibility

where platitudes disguise themselves
as knowledge
hidden in folds of borrowed centuries.

When I Give Myself to Jungles

Do I hurt language, twist or offend it
in memory's house
when it shrieks
and I will not hold its hand?

Does verbing a noun or breathing
through imprisoned breast
risk my ribcage
in this time of war and gardens?

I sleep and glyphs etched in limestone
rise beside my bed
telling stories in words I can only hear
when I give myself to jungles.

When Hopelessness Rubs Shoulders with Joy

She asks if I know about rivers,
where they begin
and how they disappear
into earth
or lose themselves in salt.

Tell me about the line, she says,
moving up and down
as water knits itself
to shore. Tell me if time
rises and falls along that rock seam.

Then she wants to know if commas
are useful in poems,
if they have a role to play
when hopelessness
rubs shoulders with joy.

She teaches me there are stories
only told in winter
when snakes sleep.
Others are summer tales,
a good cup of coffee in hand.[5]

How do I tell my story, she asks,
how do I cross the bridge
leading out and over?
Remember your name, I say,
just remember your name.

We Might Count Backward

Somewhere you just turned 87
while somewhere else
you are in your 88th year.

Or instead of each birthday
celebrating new experience,
we might count backward

from that unknown date
when our time will be up
and we reach the starting gate.

We might say *Oops, too late now*
or *Congratulations,*
it's a wrap.

And I'll still be reminding myself
to try to make her every day
the best.

The Really Bad Words

Hurt hung her head,
such bad karma.
Until *Shame* came along.
My name is worse,
she said,
I eat living flesh.

The Moment

The moment of silence begins now
but may not end
when those around you lift their eyes.

The time your loved one refused to speak
can stretch to long anguish,
no release from pain.

Childhood contained me for years,
an endless horizon
of locked doors,

then growing into myself
raced by so fast
I stumbled over body parts.

Time's sudden whispers, coughs, shudders
or slides appear without warning
to unnerve or shake the magic loose.

Approaching 80, I can make time stop
by stilling my heart
or contemplating the ravages

we leave to those who inherit our quick fix:
unstoppable war,
children who wake up hungry

in temperatures that rise through an age
where kindness takes too long
and hours climb the walls.

I am saved from smashing every clock
by knowing the young
will invent their own imperfect time.

I'll Give You a Hand

I'll give you a hand. I'm sure I have one to spare
in the tool shed where old lawn mowers
rust and throw their monthly tantrums
unable to grasp why devoted service
didn't earn them loyalty.

I'd lend you an ear though both of mine
are dulled by the screech of gunfire
reporting from any direction,
that which meant to kill
and that which believed it kept us safe.

I only have one kidney so can't offer it
in time of need. And my heart has lost
its early blush, too tired to learn
a new dance, embrace another set of loves,
give adequate service once again.

You can ask. It doesn't hurt to ask
though you must be prepared
to be turned down. And that can hurt.
My tongue? No, I'll tell you right now:
I've invested too much in my tongue

to lend it to anyone, even briefly.
You'd have to provide hard evidence
of a certain worldview,
maybe even show you intend
to leave it sharper, improve its aim.

Not the Laughter of Fun

The best poem is born in winter, comes
shivering from its thick cocoon
prepared to face bone-jarring cold
and suffocating heat
in alternate waves of meaning.

Winter Soldiers and freezing street cleaners
welcome it, beggars whose outstretched hands
are weathered purple, knees rubbed raw,
forced to ask in a world
where need is always a question in the storm.

The poem wobbles as it tries to stand,
falls as it attempts first solo flight
but feels its sinews stretch,
elbows and wrists bearing without complaint
the rigors of twisted reason.

Poems not coddled by spring effervescence
or light summer rain
have an easier time with childhood hunger,
torture, war, the horrors
humans bestow even upon our own.

They laugh—and it is not the laughter
of fun—when battered
by taunts like *pure propaganda*
meant to disparage a job well done.
Sticks and stones, they chant in unison.

The Good Book

A Good Book was inscribed on palm leaves,
another on baboon bones
or painted on cave walls thirty thousand years ago,
reproduced by Guttenberg
to broaden the reading parameter.

Remember the book where you first deciphered words,
the one that brought you perfect focus,
held memories
of your first love or last?
You still count on them to hold your hand.

Memory. Recipes. Lineages. Accounts received.
A children's book written by an adult
or by a child empowered to claim her space,
travelogue or guide, manual or memoir.
These are the good books

in gold leaf calligraphy or rows of stone glyphs
hiding within glyphs, peeking through moss
on a lintel at Tikal or Angkor Wat,
accordion codices that escaped
the fires of the Yucatán

like those brave books that hid from
the flames of Hitler's Germany
or a school board in Texas:

they stare back from beneath museum glass
or on your latest digital device.

These books preserve the secret stories
of our lives
in and between their lines
and never complain when we fall asleep
crushing their pages, dreaming their dreams.

Who Whispers, Who Interrupts

—for Ruth Hubbard

You tell me she sometimes calls at 3 in the morning
anxious because she doesn't know who she is.
You ask what she sees around her then,
try to enter her fear through familiarity,
pictures, furniture, walls.

But they aren't the right walls, those she knew
years in the house on Lakewood Avenue.
The large pot purchased at Acoma in the 1930s,
Sepik River shield or Guatemala's brilliant weave
draped across the back of a chair.

I wonder who appears in her hours of wakefulness,
who whispers, who interrupts.
Does she still try to warm herself
beside her husband's body, gone decades before,
does the path around Fresh Pond still beckon her stride?

First woman tenured in the sciences at Harvard,
assistant in her husband's lab, and when he
won Nobel glory she, who labored beside him,
went along as wife: bereft though proud.
Afterwards both left that lab

for places closer to their hearts: he to Zen, peace
and another woman, she to the roads
biology carves through female lives, a coming

together of what she had always known. He never
read her books and couldn't begin his own.

Those who love her have put her in this place,
the barren institution presumed safe,
its drooling inmates nodding in their chairs.
Far from the high four-poster bed, her own study,
space where she'd befriended colors and smells.

It's been years since we spoke on the phone,
the distant flatness in her voice
defining our last conversation:
nothing left of conspiratorial friendship,
the passion that braided our lives.

Your best friend moves deep inside herself
to a place you cannot share, though she wakes
grateful to the 3 a.m. calls. It's mostly tactile
now, she says; cuddling on hospital bed
or pushing her wheelchair toward blazing leaves.

She forgets, and I who once also called her best,
wonder who lives in that antiseptic place,
what part the woman I knew and loved,
what part someone else, stranger
to herself and the world she still inhabits.

Of Dreams and Mangled Argument

—*for Miranda Bergman*

A mother's unfailing love,
shadow shrinking into itself
as light flattens high noon.

The perfect half of a Mimbres pot
that will turn to dust if you lift it
from centuries of sand.

Pieces fall away and disappear,
sometimes with the thunder
mighty trees declare

when falling in a lonely forest,
sometimes silently
slipping from first identity.

Flesh that once supported
the rotted uniform shirt,
buttons lying in ragged formation

between skeletal ribs bleached white
from years of battlefield weather
savaged by a healing sun.

Two tiny teeth embedded in your neck
at birth, evidence of the twin
who didn't survive.

Perhaps half our lives are lived
in light, the here and now
of dreams and mangled argument.

Perhaps the messier half
will rise from the earth
when we are gone,

speak those words we hid
in secret places
or left in the open

where we thought others
heard and saw them
but were wrong.

Felix Etcetera

—for Felix Shafer

Felix etcetera moves in and out of view.
Etcetera because he is also Sarah
and Anselm, Flo, Tony and the others:
their brains gone wild
beneath the weight of this new normal.

When normal is a two-year-old shot
accidentally in her Chicago bed,
all our brains flash neon
malignant or *benign*:
erratic prognoses in real time.

No child is left behind, each war
has to be finished,
students take aim at their own
and robots replace workers
who, after all, get sick and eat.

Prison cells burst with despair.
Hope comes
in smaller and smaller packages.
Art must bear an added burden
now.

Some coils of gray may deflect the evil
while others succumb
to the tenderness of stars.
In my dream I have trouble dressing,
always come late to the table.

Each Word, Each Silence

I could go either way, she whispered,
and I knew she meant give up
or fight to live.

I could tell she wanted to understand
if I had the energy
to stand beside her,

needed to know if she could count
on me to carry
my 100 percent

to her 100 percent,
if we could continue together
in this struggle

like those we'd faced before,
pushing our love's frontier
ever outward

these magnificent years.
Each word was a monument,
each silence

the sum of every question
we'd ever asked
one another,

each promise beyond breath
or knowledge
alive in fingers intertwined.

Would she choose to succumb
among antiseptic hospital walls
or pull herself back

to the home we weave together,
return to the us of us,
that final decision

pushed ahead maybe months,
maybe years, maybe
until, our roles reversed,

I might ask the question and she
find herself reeling
before its impossible answer.

Does Being Dead Make It Hard to Keep Up?

Between Roller Coaster and Cliff Hanger
Copernicus seemed distracted.
Hard to tell if he was put off
by my twenty-first century attire
or mind's poor reach.

Both our lives straddled centuries,
his fifteenth to sixteenth,
mine twentieth to twenty-first.
But he was man, I woman,
he a scientist and I a poet.

I complimented him on discovering
our planet is not unique
in the universe, then introduced him
to the provocative multiverse
just in case being dead

makes it hard to keep up
with the latest frontiers in his field.
I thought my contribution
might get him to open up and talk
or at least join me on this carnival ride.

I told him these days we know
it all comes down
to four concepts:

matter and energy interacting
in an arena of space and time.

Not just where we are in space,
but when we are in time.
I warned we are plagued
with fundamentalists as dangerous
as the Church that threatened him.

At last he turned to look at me,
benevolent understanding
in his deep brown eyes,
right index finger pressed to lips.
He smiled.

I know, he said, but you and I
inhabit different space
in different time.
You have enough answers now,
just not enough questions.

Your Telling Detail

—*for Barbara*

We all have one, the ethnographer said,
a telling detail: how we are human.
I turn to you, memory and temperature,
know yours lives in the borderland
between silence and voice,
hangs in the tension where they meet.

Silence, suspended, is deep in you,
imprints on everything you touch,
holds its own
where another might
let careless words
trail in a dust storm of remorse.

It is there your voice emerges,
perfectly pitched
to counter every syllable lost on wind.
Your telling detail inhabits the space
between the two:
your signature, the you of you.

Why You Prefer to Travel by Road

—for Barbara

I had a place, you tell me, *a small place*
where river touches oldest rock,
I could go there for comfort
or quiet time.

It's gone now, your eyes fill
as you begin talking
about the chunks of memory
fallen out along the way.

Jagged pieces of mirror, shattered
so you view unrelated parts,
never enough
to make the picture whole.

Ephesus vanished, Nebaj undone,
the Bardo Museum in Tunis
where 23 people died today:
empty of its mosaics.

Why you prefer to travel by road,
to feel the earth unfold
beneath your feet.
Why sudden arrivals confuse.

Myopic from age ten, *my glasses **thick.***
Were your body's defenses

sparing you the horror
of a brutal childhood

or deliberate whiteout by those adults
who should have kept you safe
but tortured you instead, erasing
pieces of hard drive?

At 62 recognition is sudden, engulfing:
an artist without images
of where or when,
what came before

or after those pieces you do retain
in broken recall,
understanding disability
tethers you to your life.

She Becomes Time

—*for Barbara*

As she touches the boundary of time
she becomes time.
What is required of us at any moment,
unannounced, beyond pain or question.

As she settles against the mirror surface
she becomes a thousand versions
of herself,
every imprint she contains.

As she notices what grows between words
she moves from discomfort to terror
and back,
from breakdown to anticipation.

Her artist's hand pushes pathways
across the paper's surface,
creates spaces of silence
and spaces where secrets scream.

We grip hands so the knowing can flow
unobstructed through one to the other,
folding time and waiting
in braided fingers:

precisely here, precisely now.

Our Sad Making

Someone unexpected knocked on your door tonight,
so faintly everything you believed
brought you to your knees
before you knew what you heard was real
and moved to let him in.

He was wearing a topcoat of lies but let it drop
about his festering ankles.
Even worn white cotton socks, you thought,
elastic long undone, might have been
a gracious gesture.

But this wasn't about grace or gesture.
Pure courage almost blinded you
when the visitor sat without asking,
made himself comfortable
despite your wary silence.

What he said left slow and steady footprints
on your breastbone, tasted like
a peasant dish that didn't need desert.
No climactic scene, no highs or lows
but an invitation to keep on breathing.

Tonight you learned emotion will return, circle
your body again in excited possibility,

appear like molten lava
to unlock language and carry you
where you want to go.

You were fragile and unsuspecting when they tried
to break you with their sickness,
twisted muscle and sinew
against the grain,
played you like some cheap instrument.

But you survived. Against all odds and every prognosis
you escaped their deviant minds
and bottomless pits.
Moments of flatness a welcome exchange
for survival's song.

One day you will know warriors and resisters
both hold clues to puzzles
that always seem to have a missing piece,
a locked portal
where sun threatens to go cold.

One day you will understand liberation
and a child's secret place
as identical quests up and down the ladder,
diverted only by the simplest detour
product of our sad making.

Some Were Children

They kept coming. The building's crosscut interior
allowed me to see myself
running from window to balcony
pushing them out and off.
I watched them crash against the pavement below
only to return again: no blood, no broken limbs,
rising like boomerangs.

Some were children. I thought I would feel
a pang as I heard them fall and hit,
but they rebounded to where I kept trying
to thrust them from me, destroy them definitively.
It was never enough and I could not win
this struggle that showed no evidence
of victory on either side.

Waking from the dream did nothing to end
our ominous dance. We are locked
in each other's claim on righteousness.
Every attacker, young or old,
has been sentenced to keep on fighting,
void of feeling and trying to reclaim the power
of every story they no longer hold.

Lay Lady Lay[6]

She wears a short leather jacket
and 9-inch spike heels,
size-12 in glistening red patent leather,
carefully plucked eyebrows
on a face where pain has morphed to rage.

Lay Lady Lay, or rise and do your job.
I dream a Lady six feet tall
plus whatever it takes
for ships to discern her crown and lifted arm
in a harbor determined to welcome all.

Instead of a torch she holds a scale:
two equal trays hanging from chains
swinging in bay breeze,
describing justice.
Their contents emerge from shameful shadow.

One tray holds the barbwire fence that wept
at Matthew Shepard's last desperate plea
to live. It bleeds
beside Caster Semenya's running shoes,
all those frightened gasps for air.[7]

The other, still swinging higher,
struggles to hold identity's arc,
a family welcome mat,

warm embrace and smiles
that come before it is too late.

Lay Lady lay, why wait any longer
for the world to begin?
Do your 21st century job for those
whose passionate hearts
are unafraid to be who they are.

Writing Truth to the Power of Walls

I do not recognize this strange country
where there are no bullet holes
on buildings, no public messages
spray painted in the middle of the night
by someone risking a blast of machinegun fire
or disappearance
to an unknown cell
before the final helicopter flight.

No sudden stench of human death
impregnates earth
that gives us cherry tomatoes
and fresh basil
in this place where each
is urged to do her part
and everyone together.

Here writing truth to the power
of walls
is frowned upon.
If caught you may be fined
or forced to paint over your blasphemy.
Acting alone
helps balance
Madison Avenue graffiti
displayed to such expense and profit.

Two-Step Sonnet

—*written for* The People's State of the Union *Project*

I sit beneath the tree of promises, some
hanging dead on weighted boughs,
the mouths of others upturned
and open, hoping for rain.
Neighbors and strangers
crowd with me beneath the tree,
its shade broadens to embrace them all.

The tree of promises
promises nothing,
it is only a tree.
A girlchild with ancient eyes
leads us in song.
Everyone hears familiar language:
bones rattle down an unfamiliar scale.

Another *State of the Union* promises peace
as it secrets war, promises freedom
to those who brave desert death,
welcomes professional killers home
while deportations increase,
mourns another black youth dead,
shot by the cop who knows he has permission.

We the people have been through this
more than once. But the poem sounds,
its words create cacophonous harmony.
A century changes gender. Tomorrow says no more war.

Dear Corporate Person[8]

Dear Corporate Person: I've been told
you are no different
from the guy next door,
priest or teacher, neighbor or cop.

But let me assure you I notice the smaller box
of berries selling for the same price
as the larger one last week,
no explanation to ease the switch.

I'm not fast enough to read to the end
of the long list of possible side effects
running for one whole second
at the bottom of my TV screen,

you know, the screen where gorgeous
thirty-somethings advertise
your tooth whitener and no one suspects
Depends on streamlined hips.

You think you've convinced me fracking
is good for my soul, nuclear energy safe
and the amount of poison
found in my drinking water etcetera etcetera.

I haven't read every word of your 30-page
disclaimer, but Exploring Small Print
is the next class I mean to take
at my community Senior Center.

Dear Corporate Person: You believe
you play me for a fool, but
you'll only enjoy that bottom line of yours
as long as the earth you kill survives.

Human Conditions

One says shoes and imagines a Jimmy Choo
zinc metallic cracked leather platform
at $1,095 the pair.
In her dreams she roams Imelda Marcos' closet,
wakes wondering if this shade of gold or that of blue.
Another says shoes and stuffs the broken toes
of her only castoffs with newsprint
rescued from yesterday's gutter,
shaped by today's belief in a little good fortune.
One buys truffles, another wonders if a meal.

She saves up to get five hours beneath
her hairdresser's skilled hands.
They mold each cornrow to a head
once shamed by the words *bad hair*
now priding itself in beauty.
He sees flashing lights in his rearview mirror
and pulls to the side of the road,
knows neither argument nor expensive suit
will cut through the fear-laced rage
approaching the window he rolls down in wait.

She says no, but grandfather/uncle/date or stranger
says he knows she really wants it.
Women always do.
It's his right and she's lucky it's him,
he'll show her how it's done.

His gloating breath is the last she'll hear, as he moves on
another notch on the stock of his gun.
Or maybe it happens within the legal confines
of marriage, family and picket fence.
Fences are fences until we tear them down.

He cannot think of himself as Mary, prefers Marty,
feels wrong in the body of his birth,
gender he would shed if he could.
She stands in four-inch size 12 heels
and black leather jacket
as she explains the poem she will read
is about the wrong choice made for her at birth.

Another Time in History

For instance, the Soviet Union at the end of World War II,
twenty million souls
shoveled beneath a scarred and frozen earth.
During those plagues in the Middle Ages,
famines in China or Ireland,
wherever people depend on a growing season
making good on that promise we take for granted:
our children will have children who will have children
in a future always better than ours.
Maybe those ancestors felt as we do now.

As our temperature rises a few degrees each year,
small island nations sink beneath oceans,
polar ice caps melt and species die,
leaving irreplaceable holes in the web of life,
and those with the power to stop it
count their money and look the other way,
I think of the great grandchild
unborn because no bed exists to welcome her,
and wonder if there was another time in history
when hope was in such short supply.

Not Comforting

Friends, let me introduce myself: *Climate* here.
Both my syllables come from long lines,
prestigious roots.
Although the first has been known
to attach herself to dubious acts.

It's only lately I get paired with
that iffy word, *change*.
So uncertain, not comforting
in any way.
Believe me, we go round and round.

Ask yourself how you would like it
if every statistical message,
every mirror reflection of yourself
in polar ice cap, tornado's path
or ravaging fire showed your age.

Nowhere to hide. At this point the most I can do
is surround myself with my new best friends:
Kyoto (though he's exhausted, somewhat worse
for wear), *sustainable, committed.*
The latter folds me in her arms at night:
generous but unsure.

The Human Tree

The Jewish Holocaust lives and dies in me,
words fall short, no evocation reconnects
the broken strands of DNA.
Oh uncle erased by evil, oh aunt
whose branch on my family tree
reproduces no new green.

Oh Father who cried, oh mother
who chose make believe.
Oh witnesses filled with hope
believing it could never happen again,
we wouldn't let it happen again.
Oh underbelly of imagination gone mad.

My tree is the human tree: Armenia. Guatemala.
Rwanda. Where next?
Every branch speaking or silenced
in my voice.
No. It is not anti-Semitism
propels my rage. I refuse that trap.

Israeli teenagers posing for selfies at Auschwitz
provide a clue.
The nation of Israel running rampant
over land where Palestinians
have made their homes for centuries,
occupying territory, building settlements,

murdering youth as tender and filled with future
as those consumed in the ovens.
Accusations of anti-Semite no longer work.
And only in a world where two wrongs
are allowed to stand for right
would I have to explain this at all.

Trumping the Storyline

Two hundred eighty thousand years ago
in today's Ethiopia
a Stone Age genius
fashioned obsidian into a perfect tip
fitted to a strong shaft
and speared what we imagine
as community dinner.

The discovery astounds, yet I wait
for the wall beyond daily use
that filled our ancestors' eyes
with held breath,
explosion of stars at high noon,
the gentlest caress
or memory hurtling centuries.

Unfolding or unwinding from brains
we judge lesser because smaller,
do hidden images still wait for us
in some lost cave obscured by time?
May we still be privy
to that dazzle of passion
spread like lightning before our eyes?

Homo heidelbergensis aka Heidelberg Man
was tall and muscular: a body type
not unlike our own.

Archeologists calculate a prehistoric
assembly line.
Beneficiaries of the new technology
threw from a distance but left no evidence

of who their victims were. Wooly Mammoth?
Giant Sloth? Legged fish or a lonely band
of dinosaurs evading extinction?
We may speculate our species
older by millennia, rearrange
the branches on our family tree,
or add a talented predecessor,

but I am always waiting for evidence
of art that trumps the story line,
curls away from the need for food
or clothing, reaches to sky
to grab rainbows
and weave their colors
into a fabric that will warm us all.

Tis the Season

I'm not Christian and the date doesn't put me in a party mood
though I get the message: *'tis the season to be jolly*.
It's not that I don't love family or friends,
joyous gatherings or the glowing *luminarias*
that flicker along the rooflines of my city.
But dead children make me sad.

I avoid the malls but TV brings the holiday into my living room.
Dr. Oz prescribes and Oprah shares her Favorite Things.
As for Dr. Phil, it's mostly scams, infidelities,
and good-for-nothing adult children who live at home
and can't bring themselves to look for a job,
audiences gasp or applaud on cue.

No use dwelling on the bank that took your home
at just this time of year, interest rates tripled,
each subtle or not so subtle trick
putting more into corporate pockets,
leaving less for the needs of those who can only sweat
and pray to that infant who may have been born in Bethlehem.

Slivers of the one true cross proliferate,
too many for the wood of the original,
adorn a billion devoted breasts
—little replica instruments of capital torture—
or burn in the dark memory of a southern night,
keeping white womanhood safe.

Christmas is for the children, but don't tell that
to the daughter raped in her bedroom,
the son more familiar with his father's belt
than his embrace. Secrets and silences hover
beneath the image of family
posed on a picture-perfect greeting card: smile or else.

Hallmark has a message for any occasion: I'm Sorry,
Baptism, Bar Mitzvah or Bat, Ramadan,
Birthday, Anniversary, even Divorce.
They're up to the minute with
same-sex marriage as well as the other kind.
No need to write an original sentiment.

Poverty makes dull reading. Patriotism keeps us hating
those we are taught to hate
and loving our Christian country right or wrong.
Despite a sham separation of Church and State
the age old story stares back at us
in lights we discern from outer space.

It's all about learning to enjoy the holiday to the hilt,
get up at dawn and join the earliest shoppers,
those who come away with the biggest prize:
how much we spend revealing how much we love
and we pride ourselves
on lavish displays,

while in a land where three religions war, those whose
grandparents were forced to wear the yellow star
now light the candles and do the killing.
In Gaza Israeli bombs
strike babies in their mangers,
spreading a 21st century story of December cheer.

Unhinged from the Storyline

(you know who you are, but probably won't read this anyway)

There we wallowed, caught in our web
of misdemeanors,
streaked by shards of broken memory
unhinged from each righteous storyline.

I'd hoped we'd never have to meet again
but this afterlife
neither of us predicted or believed
had surprises for us both.

I almost retreated into my tired pattern
of ignoring the silent threats
encased in your words like secrets
crouched within undecipherable glyphs.

I guess you thought you could get away
with one more round
of knife-edged jibes
delivered in raging decibels.

And I thought I might finally convince you,
I mean now we no longer
have to worry about forever after,
but failed to grasp the terrifying reprise.

When we lived we were often warned
history repeats itself
but knew that couldn't apply to us,
unique as we believed ourselves to be.

Two Perfect Cubes

—for Barrett and Rini

"the most precious gift - the experience of knowing we always belong"

—bell hooks

You gift us two perfect cubes,
darkly glittering crystals
gleaming on their bed of pale marl.

I didn't know what they were, wondered
if natural or human-made:
such right angles, smooth planes,

so I ask, you say North African Pyrite
and I follow a cyberspace trail
to origins and formula,

chemistry I cannot decipher, peruse
fool's gold fairy tales, learn Pyrite
was a source of ignition in early firearms

and more recent destinations include
the mineral detector in crystal radios,
non-rechargeable battery cathodes,

all the way to photovoltaic panels
that may yet harness solar energy
if we give them a chance.

Like we ourselves, Iron Pyrite
is unstable in the natural environment,
always created and destroyed,

destroyed and recreated. Outcomes
like acid rain may be a danger
and as with such dangers

we would do well to keep possibility
close to the heart, allow symbol to lead
when it points to love.

All the Rest of Her Time

—for Haydée Santamaría

Her asthmatic breast was pierced
by a small staircase.
The prisoners dragged down
didn't come back up.
She heard their screams
all the rest of her time,
saw her brother's dead eye
floating in a basin
when she opened her own
searching for that sun
her Royal palms and white beach
wiped clean of memories.
Three decades later
she raised the gun
to her temple,
finished the job they left undone.
People said she was mad.

Another Night of Dreams

The elephant in the room seemed docile and clean
although immense.
I wondered what would happen
when he pooped.

I was making bread, kneading it comforted,
but became concerned
when instead of rising
the ball of dough shrank to walnut size.

My eyeglasses showed a jagged black crack
top to bottom.
I was relieved when you carefully peeled it off
with tweezers.

Another night of dreams
I want to slap upside the head.

The Story

—*for Denise Bergman*[9]

Your story is of a young girl, seven or eight,
fleeing with her pregnant mother
stopping in a roadside trench
for delivery.

It ends with the girl going for a jug
of boiling water, then stumbling,
the water scalding mother's thighs
and causing her death.

Baby also dies in this improbable tale,
impossible to erase its horror:
guilt, real or imagined, archetypal myth
of every human migration.

This is and isn't my story. You speak of your
grandmother's single blurted sentence
following years of silence
and then silence

closes around her once more,
blocking every exit,
pulling us back to a time before time,
non-linear and insistent.

One remembers blueberries trampled
underfoot.

Another holds the part where rain
comes too late for redemption.

Men place themselves at the heroic center
of this history, while women bleed
along ragged fault lines:
fault, fault, fault.

The woman I love says she's heard this before
but cannot remember where or when,
knows it comes in every color,
speaks every language,

sinks terrible roots and curls tendrils
threatening memory
that cowers buried
in every undefended throat.

A Ghost Bike Tells its Story

Down from the red and white stop sign,
in the middle of the block
a ghost bike tells its story
of loss.

Alive, the cyclist tinkered
with hand grips,
adjusted seat height,
buckled crash-proof helmet.

In death she still rides
against the wind,
waves as she passes
another cyclist on the road.

Cars enter the intersection, stop
and continue on their way.
The phantom stands at sad attention
flanked by fresh flowers,

scarves draped over handlebars,
pedals still:
another monument to one
who was loved and rode away.

Hermes Leaves His Winged Shoes

We called him Peña, Angel the given name
he rarely used:
metallurgical worker at an old factory
in Cuba's easternmost province
where iron ore turns the earth
red as those Communist Party flags
hanging limp in humid island heat.

We'd come from the capital, young poets
eager to share our work,
to lift the *ánimo* of men and women
forging a new world with broken tools,
affecting our best downhome manner,
hoping to speak their language,
to connect with the recently literate.

Peña listened then took a neatly folded sheath
of pages from his overall pocket
and as courteous response
in sonorous voice
read a poem where Hermes leaves
his winged shoes in the small shade
of a single royal palm.

I thought of Fidel's admonishment then:
Never dumb your message down
for the people
but bring the people to where
they can appreciate the greatest art:
thought and image
profound as any created.

When we got to know one another
Peña complained
people born to the luxury
of books and museums
don't know what they have, poor things,
and can afford to trivialize such riches:
condescension born of shame.

He'd never owned a typewriter,
shaped every cursive letter
with a calloused hand
by the light of a flickering candle
and his determined desire
in a one-room *bohío*
after ten hard hours of foundry work.

His poems held centuries of wisdom
and factory sweat
filtered through literacy
launched by a revolution
that wanted to change everything,
still hopes to construct a future
where Hermes travels in robust health.

A Jo Poem

A J-O-E poem, no: couldn't come up with one.
But a J-O poem, oh yes.
Jo as in *Little Women*, the sister
who wrote it all down.
Jo as in Josephine, sick grandmother
who looked on as Grandpa raped me,
something like a smile
coiled at the corner of her plaintive mouth.

Growing up as Margaret Jo and called Meg
through childhood,
I pretended inheritance of both names
from that book
loved by my friends and me,
even today refusing to acknowledge
Grandma Josephine
as namesake or legacy.

Countdown to Infinity

I sit before the computer screen
as once before paper,
wade through rage and excuse,
flee the densest regions of this market place
trying to still my mind, pay attention
only to what is here to stay,
what cannot be left behind.

Soon, if the moment is right
a color appears,
then a movement through time.
Words form from swirling dust
on a desert so vast its circumference
links past and future, strata
of Precambrian shale thundering loose.

The poem struggles to its feet,
rubs eyes closed centuries
against a startle of light,
arranges awkward extremities
upon the page.
It chooses a name for itself
and begins its countdown to infinity.

I Am Waiting

—for Lawrence Ferlinghetti, at 96,
and inspired by his poem of the same name.

I am waiting for my country
to catch up with its past,
that forgotten past
before it decided land-robs
and slave ships were good ideas.

I am waiting for my country
to stop lording it over
other countries because
they don't vote like we do
or we want their oil.

I am waiting for our keepers
of law and order to stop killing
kids because they're black,
because they wield toy guns
or fear.

I am waiting for waterboarding
to be judged as illegal as Twinkies,
a Sunday bath in Massachusetts
or gay sex in Oklahoma, Kansas,
Kentucky, Texas.

I used to wait for formidable breasts,
a graceful neck, and hair streaming

about my shoulders, not sprouting
from astonished body parts.
Too late for that.

Now I am waiting for my country
to honor poets and poetry,
send us our Christmas bonuses
because they love our poems,
Wall Street as example and mentor.

I am waiting right here right now
for a police van in rainbow hues
to roll up to the courtroom door
carrying Bush and Cheney
to the trial of their lives,

waiting for a child's face
in the crosshairs
to compel the man with the gun
to put it down
or refuse to pick it up,

where poverty, hunger, fear
of difference, and war
exist only in free museums
where teachers take children
to learn about back in the day.

I am waiting and waiting.
At 78, time is silver-blue
streaked with dark red.

I know the red will turn to blood
when 80 shrouds my shoulders.

I waited to be able to marry the woman
I love in an act more official
than the one we invented
28 years before. Impossible as
it seemed, today we have the pictures.

I waited and waited for my country
to speak to Cuba and, lo
and behold, today
they are whispering:
long-estranged lovers in a cold woods.

So I will keep waiting
as long as I'm here,
and keep on writing
these poems
with no bonus in the mail,

keep on breathing in and out,
licking the thin blanket
of melting frost
threatening to overtake
my moving lips.

Where the Human Spirit Cannot Breathe

Some must view the video, some turn away.
The prisoner kneels in orange jump suit
against sands that hide both place and time.
The masked man with British accent
wields a knife that glints in desert sun,
and promises another beheading.

Unless a prisoner exchange, unless
two hundred million in ransom,
unless, always unless.
But unless is an illusion
when atrocity reaches a place
where the human spirit cannot breathe.

Terror's job is to terrorize, and we think
there is nothing worse
than these images seducing eyes
that weep tears of blood and rage.
So soon have we forgotten Auschwitz,
Morazán, the souvenir shots at Abu Ghraib

or legal chokehold murdering Black men
on any inner city street.
Women stoned to death
or battered from girlhood through marriage
are a silent majority who suffer no less
for the permission implicit.

This is not about comparisons.
There is no such thing
as *worse than* or *as bad as*
when inhumanity is the new norm
and torture titillates, sells papers,
satisfies the cultivated taste.

Mexico

"Allá adonde no hay muerte,
allá donde ella es conquistada,
que allá vaya yo."

"There where death does not exist,
there where it has been vanquished,
that is where I will go."

—Nezahualcóyotl[10]

Through Broken Shards of Earth

—To Mexico, always dying, always rebirthing itself.

Ghosts cross my path, their voices resonate
in the conch I hold to my ear.
No tower of Babel
keeps me from their murmur,
millennial fever compressed
in this breath we share.

The woman is tunic-thin, curiosity
sparking fires inside her skull.
This *copal* air carries her off
on the wings of a dark bird.
A child's energy hits walls six-feet thick
then rebounds to trap him in his century.

On any street the amaranth of ancient stone
utters words like arrows
that hit as each sun descends
only to fly back
the following dawn,
and fade the next.

I watch their bodies move, try
to decipher their stories
echoing through broken shards of earth:
what shifting corner stones,
flawless song and the shudder
of tectonic movement leave behind.

Centuries beyond her life, Sor Juana stares at me
or Frida laughs and swings her missing leg,
Their eyes interrogate my time as I do theirs.
Men sing beneath a weight of pumice,
their chant strumming my pulse
when I fail to caress its silence.

Broken membranes separate these layers
of burning time
and faces glow in half-light.
Echoing pigments claim my memory
like 15th century flowers hold their colors
in the burial cysts, *ofrendas* all.

You who gouged them with obsidian knives,
marriage slavery
or blood that ran thick as tears,
you who sent those tanks
rolling onto a campus of active hope
or burn today's children and hide their bodies:

You are the same as they are the same
and we are the same,
finding our torturous ways
up through layers of earth and consciousness
ready to hold on and rewind
our rebel histories.

Chichén Itzá

Where crossed eyes among stone skulls
meant wisdom,
vision or a higher destiny,
where glyphs still hide within glyphs
danger and certainty walked in this jungle
twelve centuries ago.

Today vendors screech like the howlers
once leaping through these courtyards,
fake a raucous jaguar growl
on whistles made in Taiwan,
shout *cómprame cómprame*
as they push a gaudy mask at the tourist
who pleads *no money* and walks on.

Both sides of every path circling every vestige
of every pyramid or temple
are lined with stalls: men hawking
the real thing, women unfolding
colors woven of tears, their voices
rising with those of a hundred guides,

each in the center of his huddle, ears
that come from every latitude,
tourists waving their *selfie* sticks,
listening to crude tales of human sacrifice

and contorting their bodies
so the shot captures them
leaping from atop the great staircase.

Large pink umbrellas bob across the grass
shielding from midday heat
and historical exhaustion.
The guide who works eight tours a day
peppers his tale with promises:
I don't show this to everyone,
will take you where others don't go.

He dares you to believe him, wagers the ruse
may be worth an extra hundred pesos.
Chichén's dynasties of glory
now a Disneyland that draws 1.2 million
to stones that will not reveal their secrets
through the insulting din.

I think of Sir Edward dredging the sacred *cenote*
for treasure, using his diplomatic pouch
to send stolen bounty north
and Alma's campaign for return
of what belongs here:
right of occupancy, pride of place.[11]

I curl against Chaak Mool's reclining body,
meet the eyes of one hundred
braided limestone snakes,
imagine elbows and hips

blasting a small hard ball
through the ornate stone hoop,
spin my silence down sluices of time.

Could Chichén's seers have imagined
this cleaning of overgrowth
and clearing of roads,
new rules suspicious of old,
Sound & Light gaudy enough to eclipse
the sun descending like a dagger
on their calendar's perfect dawn?

Uxmal

*". . . we came at once upon a large open field
strewed with mounds of ruins, and vast buildings
on terraces, and pyramidal structures, grand and
in good preservation, richly ornamented without
a bush to obstruct the view, and in picturesque
effect almost equal to the ruins of Thebes."*

—John Lloyd Stevens[12]

Even the visitor who loved it most
evoked Old World splendor,
impossible to believe
those graceful facades
were conceived by the ancestors
of those who led him to this place.

Listen and you will hear the sounds
of wooden trumpets, conch shells,
drums and rattle,
breathe clouds of copal incense,
gaze upon the blue-green and gold
sheen of Quetzal plumes.

Ask a Dwarf, a boy not born of woman,
to build a pyramid in a single night
and don't be surprised
when that being
hatched from an iguana egg
achieves the impossible.

For here, right here, is the impossible:
Uxmal where snakes make love
on polished limestone
and feathered gargoyles
converse across patios
filled with ancient light.

Lord Chaak was first
but then Tutul Xiu
installed his family line
for generations,
and when the Spaniards arrived
allied himself with them,

which may or may not be why
this city presents itself
in such perfection,
stories we cannot bear to hear
where eyes and ears open wide
to snag storm rays from sky.

Despite the 1863 guardians
covering male genitalia
in deference to Empress Carlota,
a dance of grace and power
never stopped moving
across these walls.

Blood never stops running
from tongues pierced
by stinger rays,

rituals we don't understand
and condemn
through our prism of now.

Believe in the Dwarf, magician
whose rounded shoulders
anchor your line of sight.
Believe in Uxmal leading the *Ruta Puuc*
as it retraces its steps
through a jungle of brilliant green.

Dzibilohaltún

*After they built the churches,
there were plenty of stones
left over to build houses.*[13]

Impossible its name on my non-Maya lips,
I am welcomed by two bats
hanging against an underside of thatch
along the pathway leading in.

To the left, the presence of a single temple
(I think of Laos), The Temple
of Seven Dolls it's called
for figures found in late discovery.

Low to the ground, in perfect composure
but kept from my curiosity
by warning rope, I can only sit
and look at what remains unseen.

Then a long *sacbe*, purposeful path
takes me right where
the rounded vault of half a Christian church
still stands among Maya ruins.

Here syncretism speaks confusion's tongue,
slashes the integrity of people
destined to lose their appetite
when conquerors

make their way through mangrove swamps
between their home and an active seaport,
uninvited sails, gunpowder and germs
etching terror on hungry skin.

Xlakah *cenote* maps known time,
hides its pristine water
beneath the same lily pad cover
that murmured and moved

one thousand years before.
Tiny fish nibble at my feet
and the word for this shade of blue
suspends my disbelief.

Kabah

By three hundred years before our era,
like our first colonies
—Boston, Providence, Philadelphia—
these were great cities with histories
and differences mirrored in architecture
moving through time at its own pace.

The *sacbe* raised above the jungle floor
begins at Uxmal and 12 miles later
enters Kabah with small shells and tamped earth
imprinted on the soles of its feet,
camino real speaking a language of overgrowth
even through manicured lawn.

Kabah, Lord of the Strong and Mighty Hand,
welcomes us with serpent raised high.
He rules a temple of one thousand eyes,
round openings in stone
once red, blue, yellow at first sun,
now polished white in resignation.

Wooden lintels carved like this stone
devoured by earth and time,
Chaak masks, their long beaked noses
once confused with elephants,
point down to earth in plea for rain
or skyward in gratitude.

These buildings wear crowns, they
are regal, astonish breath,
lift memory from tranquility.
A bank of perfect stone steps
beckon me up and I follow
dragging my heart.

Among sun-bleached palaces and simple rooms
patches of shade hide in doorways
or beneath the single palm
where you, my love,
settle sketchbook on your knees,
every mystery breathing through your pen.

Labná

Its name means old or abandoned house,
a name fit for thousands of ruins
across this peninsula, some still silent
beneath thick layers of time,
others whispering their way
to a surface they claim,

their long wait never preparing us
for the monumental gate
leading nowhere but roots and branches,
jungle that's held its secrets centuries,
speaks a language
we clamor to understand.

Where the road deposits us
we say entrance,
admire embellished buildings
long and low before our startled eyes.
Frank Lloyd Wright
put his ear to this ground.

A *sacbe* takes us past three giant trees
to the back which may have been
the front: that singular gate standing
perfect and proud
with nothing before or beyond,
all honor leading nowhere
but into forest depths,
dark air,

no evidence of platforms or rooms,
only shadows tracing maps,
telling us work or fight,
eat or sleep.

What did it mean to pass through
this monumental gate
and come out the other side?
Did it beckon forward or back,
lead somewhere or nowhere
in broken memory?

Nearby a tall pyramid, cascade
of rocks, debris field
rising to perfect temple
wearing a roof comb:
open lattice whose eyes still sweep
horizons of lost time.

Today's loneliness remembers a living city
where the sound of human voices
once surged beside the jaguar's growl
and song of birds
waking familiars and others,
proclaiming where and when and how.

Labná takes me in its muscled arms,
lifts me on a draft of thin smoke
and carries me out of this life
to all those lives
that wrote my story
before I learned its incantation.

Blood Colors

White, as if memory of snow
must be the color of North.
Black is West,
lashes on brown skin holding pain
as lashes on black skin
hold a memory of future
when conquerors would replace
the labor of those they'd murdered
with slaves from across a sea.

Red names East, color of blood
spilled by enemies
and also homegrown:
brute underbelly of wisdom.
Yellow in the South
to keep us guessing
when so many clues are missing,
so many pieces disappeared
beneath the forest floor.

Green was the Center,
is still the Center:
fifth color direction grown wild
in this jungle of dizzying hues.
Unless you prefer the language
of numbers, interlocking cogs
on calendar wheels
still turning 4, 9, 13,
toward a future of blood survival.

Cuba

"Dreaming acidic green mangoes, I am.
Thinking of what will happen if...
Or, on the other hand, what will happen if not..."

—Laura Ruiz Montes[14]

Because

Because you believed you had nothing to lose
or giving your lives would mean life
for a country losing everything.
Because age followed audacity of youth.

Because you caught your oppressors off guard
and the *Sierra Maestra* took you into its heart,
wrapped you in mountain mist
and women who whispered silence:
counterpoint to big cigars and beards.

Because you wore *Orisha* beads
over mismatched fatigues,
spoke Marxism in *español*
and breathed the rhythms of *guaguancó*.

Because houses and food and medicine
and learning for everyone,
even when the word *enough* emerged
tired or redundant,
thread of opportunism
worrying the community fabric.
My cigarette ration for your cans
of sweetened milk,
my rice for your onions or *mamey*.

Because you speak politics
in the language of art
despite shameful detours
through labor camps and suicides,
subsidized poetry drawing long lines
to dusty bookstore shelves.

Because you do not forget the suicides
or those who fled on makeshift rafts
destined to die beneath waves
that pulled them down
and spit their bodies back.

In skeletal buildings peeling pale layers
of paint in tropical light,
there is always a new five-year plan,
hearts that will not submit
and memory of a man
who could speak for hours,
teaching you real history and why it mattered.

Written in *Patria o Muerte*

When night shrouds this Havana street
its buildings might be
freshly painted,
no electrical wires struggling
for power, no despair
hanging from a full moon
pale orange in duplicitous sky.

Night the great equalizer—
what we do not see
cannot make us sad.
Fifty-six years: pride
defiant against insult,
hair-trigger designed
to bring a nation to its knees.

In daylight the ragged shells
of buildings gone to age
succumb to the tropics'
sudden downpour,
claim a redemption
written in *patria o muerte*,
traded in a currency

called spirit, a future not sold
to the highest bidder,
not recognized

on any stock exchange
or designed to dominate
and kill.
We live in community, or die.

Imaginary Telescope

Rocking chairs sway at funerals
and on shadowy verandas,
stained fabric cones
drip dark coffee into small cups,
hologram of the family departed.

White cherimoya flesh spits its
black seeds off the tongue.
Black rhythm of skin drawn taut
across wooden drums
coursing through chameleon blood.

They sing of your palms and beaches,
a history where clean brows
outsmart every sleight of hand
or other inconvenient truths
and dignity screams from billboards

while I focus the skittish lens of my
imaginary telescope, trying
to remember . . . remember . . .
small animal curled beneath my skin
returning with each new season.

Far Side of Utopia

If Memory says it's tired, needs to stop
for a moment and take a break,
remind it of bridges and tunnels,
dangerous byways
and passages
where water threatens blood
all the way home.

When Memory is tricked or battered
its maturity suffers.
Something is lost forever
between the hand's warm touch
and temperature of air
as spring settles into summer
and winter remains a distant threat.

Memory breathes down your neck
even when extraneous voices
jostle from all sides
weaving false narratives.
Speeches will be made,
books written and histories stamped
with official seals of approval.

She will find you by instinct,
know you by scent
or feel,

identify your solid contours
in the shiver of her dignified spine,
depth of breath
and reach of fingertips.

And you will recognize her presence,
invite her into that place
where a child utters his first word,
poetry proclaims its relevance,
and cause and effect
curl into one another,
far side of utopia.

Your Intimate Heart

Waves power across the *malecón*,
crash against bare legs,
proud barrier, tired asphalt:
threat of blue death
or yellow fortune.

Yearly, young hands release flowers
in Camilo's memory,[15]
hands that reach for a perfect nation
or greener grass:
rainbow dreams either way.

Black *Abakuá*, white law,
color of time and space,
memories of a period called gray
each time fear poisons brilliance
on the edge of the censor's blade.

Color as question mark, *radio bembá*
running rampant
between desire and possibility,
when *may* becomes *must*
and rebellion scatters the blood.

Some speak only of those who left,
others of those who want
to come home,
while those who are here to stay
commune with your intimate heart.

When Justice Felt at Home

Something has changed.
Only old friends,
those who shared split peas
and white rice
on sweltering Havana nights
still call me *compañera*:
sweet designation
meaning comrade or friend
lover or familiar
in those luminous days
when justice felt at home
in our desire.

Now, more often than not,
it's *señora*:
regression to a prehistory
when married or single
young or old
mattered most.

Still, *compañera* and *compañero*
are indelibly embossed
on the swaying trunks of Royal Palms,
in Sierra Maestra granite
and along the dissembling coastline
of an Island that still shouts freedom
into gale-force winds.

The Future of Poetry is Safe

—*for Jude Marx*

The young ones recite from memory
laugh at our labels
as they carry our discoveries
and hard-won victories
into verb's future
with a confidence we built
line by tentative line.

I don't get the slam rules or voting,
too much a part
of that commodity scene
I've fought all these slow-turning years,
but when she digs beneath English
and finds Hebrew, Russian, salt spray

like dark waves against the side
of a lonely ship,
when she writes she wants
to grow facial hair
so she can walk around clean-shaven
or is frightened of corsets
and so frightened too of whale bones and oceans,

I know the future of poetry is safe.

Notes

1. *The Putterer's Notebook* by Alkilah Oliver, Belladona Books, New York City. The quotes are from different parts of the book, unrelated to one another.

2. *On Lies, Secrets, and Silence: Selected Prose 1966-1978* by Adrienne Rich, W. W. Norton, New York, 1979. pp. 13-14.

3. On October 2, 1968 thousands of students and others involved in Mexico's student movement gathered at the Plaza of Three Cultures, Tlatelolco, in the center of Mexico City. The government and paramilitary forces attacked the crowd from land and air. Estimates of those killed range from 300 to more than 1,000, though the official government count at the time was 26.

4. *The Elegant Universe: Superstrings, Hidden Dimensions, and the Quest for the Ultimate Theory* by Brian Greene, W. W. Norton, New York, 1999.

5. The Navajo or Diné people are among those who have stories that can only be told in certain seasons.

6. Bob Dylan song.

7. Matthew Shepard (1976 –1998) was a young gay American student at the University of Wyoming who was beaten, tortured, and tied to a fence near Laramie on the night of October 5, 1998, and died six days later at a hospital in Fort

Collins. Mokgadi Caster Semenya (1991) is a South African middle-distance runner and world champion who won gold in the women's 800 meters at the 2009 World Championship. Following that victory she was subjected to gender testing and withdrawn from international competition until a year later when she was deemed "a woman" and cleared to return to the sport in her gender category.

8. In its 2012 case *Citizens United v. Federal Election Commission*, the US Supreme Court held that corporations have the same rights as individuals.

9. I heard this story from Denise, who has written it much more fully in *The Telling* (Červaná Barva Press, Somerville, Massachusetts, 2014).

10. Nezahualcóyatl (1402-1472) was an architect, philosopher, poet, warrior, and ruler of the ancient Mexican city of Texcoco. His name means Coyote Who Fasts. He is best remembered for his poetry, but according to accounts by his descendants and biographers, Fernando de Alva Cortés Ixtlilxochitl and Juan Bautista de Pomar, he had an experience of meeting an "Unknown, Unknowable Lord of Everywhere" to whom he built an entirely empty temple in which no blood sacrifices of any kind were allowed —not even those of animals. Fragment translated by MR.

11. Over more than a decade Sir Edward Thompson, US consul in Yucatán, dredged Chichén Itzá's sacred *cenote* and sent its treasures via diplomatic pouch to the Peabody Museum at Harvard University. Alma Reed, reporting for the

New York Times, gained Thompson's confidence. She wrote and documented an article published under her byline in the *Times' Sunday Magazine* of April 4, 1923 and expanded into another requested by *The New York World* on April 22. Mexico demanded the return of its patrimony or the sum of two million dollars. The Peabody eventually did return much of what it had come by illegally. Reed was also influential in getting *The Times* and other important US newspapers to editorialize in favor of the United States recognizing the Obregon government. See *Peregrina: Love and Death in Mexico* by Alma M. Reed (University of Texas Press, Austin, 2007) for the fascinating life story of the woman engaged to marry Felipe Carillo Puerto, socialist governor of the state of Yucatán who was executed days before their marriage was to take place. Reed was one of a number of US American women who made important contributions to Mexico.

12. Incidents of Travel in the Yucatán, 1843.

13. Diego de Landa, paraphrase.

14. Cuban poet (Matanzas, Cuba 1966). From "Acidic Fruit" in the book of the same name. Translation MR.

15. Camilo Cienfuegos was one of the heroes of the Cuban revolution. He was lost early on, in a plane crash at sea on October 28, 1959, and every year on that date Cuban school children toss flowers into the water in his memory.

Acknowledgments

A few of these poems, sometimes in slightly different versions, first appeared in *Antropocene*, *Casa de las Américas* (in Spanish translation by Ana Puñal), *Feminist Formations*, *Fixed and Free Poetry Anthology 2015*, *Helix Syntax* (Literary Magazine of the 41st Summer Writing Program, Jack Kerouac School of Disembodied Poetics, Naropa University), The Literary Journal of the *Kurt Vonnegut Memorial Library*, *Literal*, *Malpais Review*, *Mas Tequila Review*, *Mo' Joe The Anthology*, *Napalm Health Spa*, *Poet Lore*, *Prairie Schooner*, *Santa Fe Literary Review*, and *Voices de la Luna*.

About the Author

Margaret Randall is a feminist poet, writer, photographer and social activist. She is the author of over 100 books. Born in New York City in 1936, she has lived for extended periods in Albuquerque, New York, Seville, Mexico City, Havana, and Managua. Shorter stays in Peru and North Vietnam were also formative. In the 1960s, with Sergio Mondragón she founded and co-edited *El Corno Emplumado / The Plumed Horn*, a bilingual literary journal which for eight years published some of the most dynamic and meaningful writing of an era. Robert Cohen took over when Mondragón left the publication in 1968. From 1984 through 1994 she taught at a number of U.S. universities.

Randall was privileged to live among New York's abstract expressionists in the 1950s and early '60s, participate in the Mexican student movement of 1968, share important years of the Cuban revolution (1969-1980), the first four years of Nicaragua's Sandinista project (1980-1984), and visit North Vietnam during the heroic last months of the U.S. American war in that country (1974). Her four children—Gregory, Sarah, Ximena and Ana—have given her ten grandchildren and one great-grandchild. She has lived with her life companion, the painter and teacher Barbara Byers, for the past 29 years.

Upon her return to the United States from Nicaragua in 1984, Randall was ordered to be deported when the government invoked the 1952 McCarran-Walter Immigration and Nationality Act, judging opinions expressed in some of her books to be "against the good order and happiness of the United States." The Center for Constitutional Rights defended Randall, and many writers and others joined in an almost five-year battle for reinstatement of citizenship. She won her case in 1989.

In 1990 Randall was awarded the Lillian Hellman and Dashiell Hammett grant for writers victimized by political repression. In 2004 she was the first recipient of PEN New Mexico's Dorothy Doyle Lifetime Achievement Award for Writing and Human Rights Activism.

Recent non-fiction books by Randall include *To Change the World: My Life in Cuba* (Rutgers University Press), *More Than Things* (University of Nebraska Press), *Che On My Mind,* and *Haydée Santamaría, Cuban Revolutionary: She Led by Transgression* (both from Duke University Press). "The Unapologetic Life of Margaret Randall" is an hour-long documentary by Minneapolis filmmakers Lu Lippold and Pam Colby. It is distributed by Cinema Guild in New York City.

Randall's most recent collections of poetry and photographs are *Their Backs to the Sea* (2009) and *My Town: A Memoir of Albuquerque, New Mexico* (2010), *As If the Empty Chair: Poems for the disappeared / Como si la silla vacía: Poemas para los desaparecidos* (2011), *Where Do We Go From Here?* (2012), *Daughter of Lady Jaguar Shark* (2013), *The Rhizome as a Field of Broken Bones* (2013), and *About Little Charlie Lindbergh and other Poems* (2014), all published by Wings Press.

For more information about the author, visit her website at www.margaretrandall.org.

Colophon

This first edition of *She Becomes Time*, by
Margaret Randall, has been printed on 55
pound Edwards Brothers "natural" paper con-
taining a percentage of recycled fiber. Titles
have been set in Nueva type, the text in
Adobe Caslon type. This book was designed
by Bryce Milligan.

On-line catalogue and ordering:
www.wingspress.com
Wings Press titles are distributed to the trade by the
Independent Publishers Group
www.ipgbook.com
and in Europe by Gazelle
www.gazellebookservices.co.uk

Also available as an ebook.